ANGER MANAGEMENT
Workbook for Kids

ANGER MANAGEMENT
WORKBOOK for KIDS

50 Fun Activities to Help Children Stay Calm and Make Better Choices When They Feel Mad

SAMANTHA SNOWDEN, MA

Foreword by Andrew Hill, PhD

Illustrations by Sarah Rebar

ALTHEA
PRESS

For general information on our other products and services or to obtain technical support, please contact our Customer Care Department within the United States at (866) 744-2665, or outside the United States at (510) 253-0500.

Althea Press publishes its books in a variety of electronic and print formats. Some content that appears in print may not be available in electronic books, and vice versa.

Cover Designer: Katy Brown
Interior Designer: Patrick Barber and Alyssa Nassner
Editor: Katharine Moore
Production Editor: Erum Khan

Illustrations © Sarah Rebar, 2018

ISBN: Print 978-1-64152-092-8 | eBook 978-1-64152-354-7

A while ago, I was shown the great joy that comes from dedicating one's merit to guiding teachers and loved ones. I would like to dedicate this workbook to all the parents out there who continue to show the profound love of which humans are capable. I would like to thank all of my teachers, who continue to share great depths of wisdom with me.

Above all, I dedicate this workbook to my mother, Melissa, who lives as an angel among mere mortals, spreading love, gratitude, and infinite optimism wherever she goes.

Contents

• •

Part 1 Why Do I Feel Angry?

Part 2 What Happens When I Feel Angry?

Part 3   What Should I Do with My Anger?

Foreword

• •

WE ARE ALL RESPONSIBLE FOR OUR ACTIONS, but what about managing our thoughts and feelings? We often develop the skills of noticing, identifying, and responding to our emotions because we have to, not because we had great teachers early in life. But we have the power to improve those emotional regulation skills. Most people—even kids—can make a great deal of change in how happy and safe they feel by learning to understand their feelings instead of simply reacting to their emotions. As we develop a sense of control and reduce our reactivity to our thoughts and emotions, this also helps us more skillfully react to the environment and the emotions of others around us.

Kids are not simply tiny humans, and they have greater emotional needs for safety and security than they might later in life. They are extremely sophisticated in understanding that they are not happy, that something makes them feel bad, or that they don't like something. They don't have the agency or control over their environment that many adults do; but developing an understanding of their own minds, hearts, and reactions is a skill that will provide this agency, along with many lifelong benefits. As a kid in the 1970s with a lot of my own fear and anger, I wish someone had given me a book like this to help provide a framework for me to start getting a handle on the emotional discomfort every kid goes though.

With this workbook, Samantha Snowden has provided a rich and useful set of practices to help develop the skills to notice and manage our internal states. Once kids start to develop a sense of freedom from their own emotions—not by ignoring them or pushing them away, but by validating the processes and circumstances that are creating them—great self-regulation skills can start to develop.

I have worked with Samantha Snowden for many years in multiple health and wellness contexts. She is always the kids' favorite mindfulness teacher, bringing compassion, care, and humor to every teaching interaction. She has given a great deal to the clients and friends we share, and I was delighted to be asked to write this foreword to her book, *Anger Management Workbook for Kids*.

The exercises and readings that follow will help kids of all ages break through the habit of automatic reactions, provide tools for labeling and understanding how their anger and discomfort work, and support them on the path of learning to be comfortable with their own emotions. This will help kids act quickly and skillfully from those emotions and be less driven by fear and anger.

—ANDREW HILL, PhD
  Founding Director of the Peak Brain Institute and UCLA Lecturer in Psychology

A Letter to
GROWN-UPS

HELLO!

In over 10 years of working with families, I have learned that anger can be one of the biggest obstacles to harmony. I see families stuck in cycles of frustration around certain situations, like transitioning from school to home, playing video games, or going to bed.

I hope this workbook helps open the lines of communication and connection so your family feels united as you work toward common goals of understanding, cooperation, and self-awareness.

You can work on these activities with your child, or your child can work on them alone. When you explore the activities together, I encourage you to bring curiosity and a willingness to discover not only your child's angry tendencies, but also your own, free from blame or judgment. As you open up about your own experiences with anger, your child will feel more comfortable being vulnerable and will see that anger is an emotion that everyone feels.

This workbook addresses the following topics:

- Identifying habits and trends of anger
- Recognizing how anger feels
- Understanding what triggers anger
- Communicating feelings, needs, and wants
- Cultivating self-kindness, joy, and appreciation

These activities are designed to help children get to know their anger habits with openness and kindness. Once they identify their habits and their likely consequences, further activities cultivate more pleasant states of being through gratitude, friendliness, and self-kindness.

May your experience with this process be enjoyable, illuminating, and provide relief.

Warmly,

Samantha

A Letter to
KIDS

• •

ANGER IS A DIFFICULT FEELING. It makes us want to destroy things and say hurtful things we later regret. When we look back at what we said and did when we felt angry, we feel sorry and wish we had done things differently. This book will help you see anger in a new way. Instead of acting out of anger or pushing it away, you will get curious about anger and allow it to pass before it gets out of control.

This workbook is a safe place to learn more about yourself, try out new activities, and make new habits that will help you be happier, calmer, and more in control when you feel angry.

As you explore the activities in your workbook, you may want to ask an adult to practice with you and talk with you about what you notice. Always remember that we all feel angry sometimes and that when you feel upset, you are not alone. There are people around you who want to help you feel better.

I hope this book helps you feel happier, friendlier, and safer when things get tough.
Warmly,

Samantha

PART 1

Why Do I Feel Angry?

What We'll Learn

Figuring out what makes us angry can be a little tricky. Anger seems to come out of nowhere, and sometimes when we least expect it. Some of us get angry around certain people, and others get angry when going to certain places. When we are unsure when anger will show up or what our anger is like, it is much harder to know what to do.

This section introduces you to anger. You'll learn more about when anger may visit and how it makes you and other people feel. Using your curiosity, you can get to know your habits better, like a scientist discovering something new by looking at it with a microscope. Thinking about your anger habits will help you see patterns more clearly and find healthy ways to feel calm again.

Understanding *why* you feel angry and how it affects your friends and family will help you make better choices *when* you feel angry.

THIS IS HOW ANGER FEELS

Imagine you are a detective. Detectives find clues and solve mysteries. In this section, the mystery you will solve is how your anger feels and how to recognize and describe it.

Every day there are many things we must do and people we must be around. If we are not in the mood to do something, like go to school, do our homework, or share with friends, we can feel frustrated, annoyed, and angry.

What do you do when you are angry? You may scream or cry or even throw things. By taking the time now, while you are calm, to find clues about what makes you angry, you will be able to choose different ways of acting when you feel angry.

You will also learn to pay attention to the clues your body gives you that you are starting to feel upset, and you'll be able to describe them. Your body lets you know it's angry by speeding up your heartbeat, heating you up, or making you feel like you want to break or smash something.

Let's solve the mystery of anger.

Say Hi to Your Anger

When we feel angry, it is natural to want to make the feeling go away as quickly as possible, especially when we feel like we lose control of ourselves. However, when we use curiosity to get to know anger, we welcome the feeling instead, as though offering the difficult visitor some tea and cookies.

Take some time to get to know what your anger is like. As you think about your answers to the following questions, close your eyes and imagine all the different parts of anger. When you are done, you can draw a picture of you welcoming and getting to know your anger.

What does anger look like? _____

_____

What does anger smell like? _____

_____

What does anger sound like? _____

_____

What does anger feel like? _____

_____

Say Hi to Your Anger, *continued*

If anger was a character from a book or TV show, it would be: _

_ _

A motto is something a character says a lot. It represents their personality and what they're about. If your anger had a motto, what would it be?

_ _

Take a few minutes to write a letter to your anger. Here are a few lines to start you off. Feel free to make your letter as long as you would like.

LETTER TO ANGER

Hi Anger, my name is _ .

If you had a color it would be _ .

I notice you most when _ .

I would like to get to know you a little bit better. _

_ _

_ _

_ _

Now that you've gotten to know your anger, draw a picture of what it looks like when it comes to visit.

Naming Our Emotions

Anger is a difficult emotion that can make us want to do something quickly, without thinking first. We react this way because of the part of our brain called the *amygdala* (pronounced ah-mig-dah-la), which turns on when we have a big emotion like anger. The amygdala is like an alarm going off in the brain. This is helpful when you touch a hot stove, for instance, because you will get burned if you don't move away fast. Our ancestors needed to react quickly because predators such as lions and tigers could eat them if they weren't paying attention.

The world we live in now is very different from that time, but we still have that part of our brain. It can make us want to fight or destroy things when anger comes around.

Luckily, we also have another part of our brain called the *prefrontal cortex*, or PFC. This part of the brain gives us the ability to pause before we react, and to think of the consequences our actions will have for others. When we use the PFC to name an emotion like anger, it is like applying the brakes on a fast-moving train.

We help ourselves by pausing and thinking about the feelings moving through us. This calms the part of the brain that reacts quickly (the amygdala) by turning on the more responsible part of the brain (the PFC).

It helps to learn the right words so we can get better at understanding and explaining just what we feel.

Below you will find some words that describe different types of uncomfortable feelings. Read them to yourself or aloud to an adult, and ask for help with words you don't know yet.

FEELING WORDS FOR DIFFICULT MOODS

- Angry
- Careless
- Cranky
- Frustrated
- Impatient
- Irritated
- Rushed
- Sad
- Tired
- Worried

Imagine yourself in the following situations, then find one or two feelings from the word list that may come up in each of those situations. Write the feeling words down. Then add a situation of your own and write in a feeling word that describes how you feel in that moment.

When I leave for school in the morning, I feel _____

_____ .

When I am waiting to be picked up after school, I feel _____

_____ .

When I am late to a party or to play with friends, I feel _____

_____ .

When I share a toy when I don't want to, I feel _____

_____ .

When I don't sleep well because of bad dreams, I feel _____

_____ .

When I _____ ,

I feel _____

_____ .

How Does My Body Feel?

When we pause to notice our body sensations, our anger slows and starts to fade. It may be easy to notice how we feel when we get hurt or are really hungry, but there are many other body sensations that give us clues that something needs our attention. When we notice our sensations and name them, the wiser part of our brain (the PFC) turns on and we can soothe the reactive part of our brain (the amygdala).

Close your eyes and think back to a time when you were angry. Can you remember how you could tell you were angry from the clues your body gave you?

Use the sensation words below and your own words to identify the sensations you feel in your body when you feel angry, then draw them on the diagram. You can also use colors, shapes, and other drawings to show how anger feels for you.

SENSATION WORDS

- Dark
- Dizzy
- Fast breathing
- Fast heartbeat
- Hard to breathe
- Heavy
- Hollow
- Hot
- Nauseous
- Numb
- Tight
- Tingly
- Shaky
- Sharp
- Warm

THIS IS WHAT ANGER DOES

When we feel angry, we feel out of control. It is hard to control our body, our thoughts, and our words. For example, we may fall to the floor and kick and punch, think that we hate someone we really love, or scream and cry.

Anger makes a lot of our thoughts appear more intense to match the intensity of the anger we feel. It can be difficult to notice while it is happening, but when you are calm, it is easier to think about what anger does.

When you are relaxed it is also a good time to think about how you respond to anger and how your angry actions affect others. The things we do and say when we feel angry can scare or upset those we love. Friends may not want to play with us, or we may get in trouble at school. Think about the consequences of your angry words and actions. Thinking about the consequences will encourage you to find better ways of dealing with your anger.

What Happens in Your Brain and Body When You Feel Angry

When we are angry, our body usually feels a lot of energy. It is as though our body and mind are screaming, "Do something!" Anger tells the body to act, and many bodily changes happen to help us act. You may notice some of these feelings in your body: your muscles tensing, your heart beating faster, and your belly feeling tight.

DEFINITION OF TERMS

Amygdala: Our emotional alarm system, which tells the body to fight danger, run from it, or freeze.

Prefrontal cortex: Calms the amygdala by naming our feelings and imagining the consequences of our actions.

Adrenaline: A chemical in our body that gives us the energy to do something fast.

When we have a big emotion like anger, the amygdala fires. Then adrenaline flows throughout the body, making the body want to do something quickly. The prefrontal cortex then comes in to help. It puts the brakes on by identifying our feelings and body sensations.

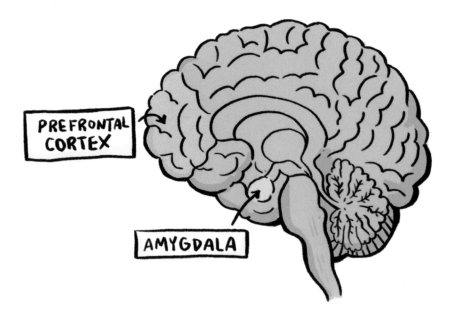

What Happens in Your Brain and Body When You Feel Angry, *continued*

What does your amygdala tell you to do when you're angry?

Example: "You should break your brother's Lego building!"

What does your prefrontal cortex tell your amygdala in order to put the brakes on your angry urges?

Example: "Wow! You are very angry. I can tell because your face is hot and you have a lot of energy in your body."

Decoding Our Anger

Now we know why anger makes us want to do certain things. Let's explore the different kinds of urges we feel when angry. It is important to remember to decode our anger when we are calm, so we don't get angrier by being hard on ourselves.

As you look over the list of urges, think about which ones you have most often. Then fill in your top five instincts and describe a time you have felt each one.

URGES

- Bullying (teasing, spreading rumors, and name-calling)
- Destroying something (breaking toys or furniture)
- Having a tantrum (screaming and punching)
- Ignoring people
- Losing control of my body (kicking and screaming on the floor)
- Making threats ("I won't be your friend ever again!")
- Moving too quickly (running or crashing into something)
- Punishing someone (refusing to answer them, call them back, or invite them to an event)
- Slamming doors
- Thinking of ways to get revenge (wanting to hurt someone who has hurt you)
- Using foul language (using words you know upset people)
- Using words to hurt someone's feelings (saying unkind things to someone)

Example: I feel like *yelling or crying* when *my mom tells me to stop playing video games.*

I feel like _____

when _____ .

I feel like _____

when _____ .

Decoding Our Anger, *continued*

I feel like _____

when _____.

I feel like _____

when _____.

I feel like _____

when _____.

I feel like _____

when _____.

Consequences of Acting Out

Saying or doing something out of anger can have some big consequences. Some of the consequences may affect how people feel or how they treat us or act around us. Other consequences may include having our favorite things or privileges taken away, or not being able to go places we like. On the next page, you'll find a list of some of the possible consequences of anger.

Name a place where you felt angry: _

_ _

What did you do when you felt angry? _

_ _

What were the consequences of your actions (like punishment, making others angry, or sadness)?

_ _

Name a person you were angry with: _

Why were you angry with them? _

_ _

What were the consequences? _

_ _

SOME CONSEQUENCES OF ANGER

- Feeling frightened
- Feeling unsafe
- Getting in trouble at school
- Losing others' trust
- Not being able to go places we like
- Others getting angry or embarrassed
- Punishments (having things taken away, like video games or privileges)

HOW TO LOOK OUT FOR ANGER

Can you think of ways to be prepared for something going wrong? We have first aid kits in case we get hurt. We pack snacks in case we get hungry. To be prepared for anger, we get to know our anger habits. To get to know anger, it's helpful to ask ourselves *who* we get angry around, *what* makes us feel angry, and *when*, *where*, and *why* we get angry.

Who do we get angry around? Some people are just harder to get along with. Sometimes friends have a hard time sharing, or don't know how to tell you what they need. They may bother you by not listening or forget to include you in a game. Knowing which people are harder to be around can help you feel prepared before you start to feel angry with them.

What makes us angry? Everyone has something that really bothers them. Some people get angry when something unusual happens or when they can't get an ice cream at the store. Others are angered by hurtful words or putdowns. When we know what makes us angry, we can be prepared to respond in a healthier way.

Before we react to our anger, it is helpful to know what causes it. There are a few basic triggers for anger that all humans share. They include:

Feeling physically unsafe

Feeling stuck or stopped from doing something we want to do

Having our stuff taken away

Insults

Someone not respecting our personal space

Unkindness shown to friends or family members

When we see rules being broken

When you recognize the trigger for your anger, it helps your prefrontal cortex come online to make sense of why you feel angry.

When do we feel angry? During certain times of day, we are more likely to feel cranky and angry. Many of us feel angry when we are hungry, tired, or bored. We may even be more likely to feel angry after a change, like coming back from a vacation or when a friend goes home after playing at our home.

Where does it happen? Anger can strike anywhere. However, there are some places where it is more likely to come up. For you, it may be the dentist's office or at school during a part of the day like recess or math time.

Why does anger happen? As we are finding out, anger can come up for many reasons. It happens when something isn't going our way, or because we are disappointed by not getting what we want. Whatever the reason may be, curiosity can help solve the mystery of our anger habits. It can also help us find ways to be ready to handle anger.

Understanding our habits allows us to adjust so we can take care of ourselves. We can do this by doing calming activities. We can also ask an adult for help.

Where and When Does My Anger Show Up?

Anger can sneak up on us. It can happen quickly and in places where there are other people. It can be hard to calm down if anger surprises us.

If we think back to times when we felt angry, we can be better prepared to calm ourselves when we are in a similar situation again.

PLACES WHERE IT HAPPENS

Here are some places where anger may show up. As you think about each place, remember a time you felt angry in that place and write about it. You can write down an angry thought you get sometimes or something that happens that makes you angry.

IN THE CAR

AT SCHOOL

AT HOME

AT THE PLAYGROUND

AT THE STORE

TIMES WHEN IT HAPPENS

Here are some times when anger may show up. Write a little bit about how anger may appear at each of these times and what some of the consequences have been.

How does anger show up during homework time? _

_ _

What are the consequences? _

_ _

How does anger show up during playtime with friends? _

_ _

How do friends react? _____

_____

How does anger show up at bedtime? _____

_____

How does this affect your sleep or energy in the morning? _____

_____

Do you ever get angry when Mom or Dad says no? _____

_____

What happens when you don't accept their no? _____

_____

Write down one other time you got angry and what consequences it had for you and other people.

_____

_____

_____

Anger Thermometer

When something triggers our anger, we can go from calm to furious in a few seconds.

Sometimes big feelings like anger creep up on us and get more intense quickly, like a pot of water boiling over. It is hard to notice the steps along the way that make anger get hotter. When anger gets too hot, it is hard to remember and practice our self-soothing tools.

This activity will help you identify *what* brings anger up for you.

ANNOYED ZONE

First, think of a time when you were slightly annoyed. Remember the triggering places and times you identified in Activity 1 in this section. Write down three examples of people or experiences that annoy you.

How did you know you were annoyed? What were the body clues that let you know you were getting annoyed? Write down the clues (body sensations or thoughts you noticed) at levels 1, 2, and 3 in the Annoyed Zone.

EXAMPLE

1. Sitting in the car during traffic
2. My little brother interrupting me
3. Mom telling me I can't have more cookies

Clue 1. Start swinging my legs
Clue 2. Start whining
Clue 3. Forehead wrinkles up

1. _   **Clue 1.** _

2. _   **Clue 2.** _

3. _   **Clue 3.** _

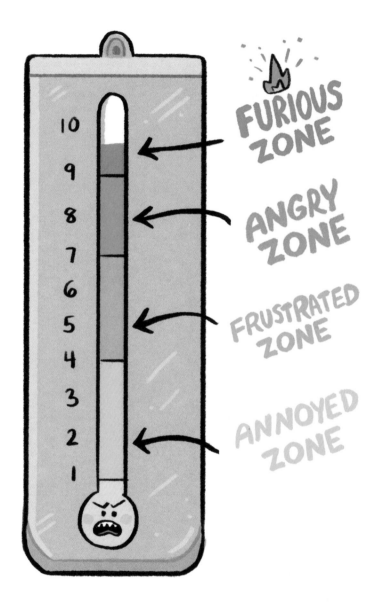

FRUSTRATED ZONE

What about when you are frustrated? Think of three times you were frustrated, write them down, and try to remember the clues your body gave you. Did you raise your voice or feel your face scrunching up?

4. _____   Clue 4. _____

5. _____   Clue 5. _____

6. _____   Clue 6. _____

ANGRY ZONE

When were you angry? How did you know when you were in the Angry Zone? Did you start to yell? Did you feel like hitting or kicking? Did you cry?

7. _____   Clue 7. _____

8. _____   Clue 8. _____

FURIOUS ZONE

If you were a cartoon character, you might have steam coming out of your ears at this point. Think about two times when you were the angriest you've ever been. What did you do or say? Can you remember how your body felt?

9. _ Clue 9. _

10. _ Clue 10. _

If we can catch anger before it gets raging hot, we can choose a better way to deal with it.

We All Get Angry Sometimes

Anger is a feeling all humans have sometimes. It is a feeling that has been passed down from our ancient ancestors for some good reasons.

For example, anger helps us know when we really care about something or someone. This can be the anger we feel when we are protective of a loved one who is threatened.

Anger also puts us on alert to protect our bodies if we sense any physical dangers. However, these days we don't have large animals like tigers and bears chasing us, like our ancestors did. The angering situations we now face don't require us to fight; instead, we need to think clearly about what to do and the consequences of our actions.

Let's look again at things that tend to make all of us angry sometimes. Next to each example, write about a time you faced that situation.

FEELING PHYSICALLY UNSAFE

I felt physically unsafe when _____

_____ .

FEELING STUCK OR STOPPED FROM DOING SOMETHING WE WANT TO DO

When has this happened to you? _____

_____

HAVING OUR STUFF TAKEN AWAY

Who took something from you? What did they take? _____

_____

INSULTS

This insult makes me angry: _____

SOMEONE NOT RESPECTING OUR PERSONAL SPACE

Who doesn't respect your personal space? _____

UNKINDNESS SHOWN TO FRIENDS OR FAMILY MEMBERS

When was someone unkind to a friend or family member? _____

_____

WHEN WE SEE RULES BEING BROKEN

Someone broke the rules when _____

_____.

What is something you understand better about yourself because of thinking about your anger?

_____

_____

How do you feel after learning that anger helps us understand ourselves better? _____

_____

WHERE DOES THE ANGER GO?

Anger creates a lot of energy in our bodies. It can feel like a tornado moving through, leaving a mess behind. When we feel angry, we often feel strong urges to do something physical, like kick, punch, or scream. After we have acted on our anger and all the energy has moved through us, other feelings come up. We can feel tired or shaky. We may feel sad, confused, relieved, or guilty for what we said or did.

Our anger affects other people, too. Our family and friends may feel confused about what made us angry, or they may feel sad that we said something hurtful to them. If Mom or Dad was around when we were angry, they might have felt worried for us or upset that we broke something or said something mean.

It is important to think about the effects our anger has on us *and* the people we care about. We don't do this to be hard on ourselves for getting angry. We do it to show ourselves kindness and understanding so we can find better ways of acting next time.

When we remember how our anger affects other people, we naturally want to try to do something different. This is because we care for our family and friends and want them to feel safe.

In the next activities, you'll think about times you've been angry. You'll get to know how you feel in your body and mind after anger passes. You will also imagine how other people think and how they feel when you are angry.

This understanding will encourage you to meet your anger with friendliness and understanding, so you and the people you care about feel safe, calm, and willing to help.

After Anger Passes: Body

After the storm of anger passes, we feel many sensations in our body. Once we get to know these effects, we can find other, more helpful behaviors instead of letting the storm of anger sweep through us.

Close your eyes and think about a time you were very angry. Think about what you did. Did you scream, hit, or break something? Now think about how your body felt once the anger passed. Were you tired, shaky, or numb?

In the blank space, write a sensation you felt when anger had passed. Choose from the list of sensation words or use your own words. Then draw a picture of how you felt.

SENSATION WORDS

- Hot/Cold
- Numb
- Restless

- Shaky
- Slow/Fast breathing
- Tingly

- Tired
- Tummy ache
- - - - - - - - - - - - - - - - - - -

Now, draw another picture showing what you usually want after anger passes. Choose from the list or from your own thoughts.

WHAT DO YOU WANT AFTER ANGER PASSES?

- A hug
- Be alone
- Cry

- Take a bubble bath
- Talk to someone
- Watch a movie

- _ _ _ _ _ _ _ _ _ _ _ _ _ _ _ _
- _ _ _ _ _ _ _ _ _ _ _ _ _ _ _ _
- _ _ _ _ _ _ _ _ _ _ _ _ _ _ _ _

After Anger Passes: Body, *continued*

Finally, draw a picture of an urge you have when your anger has passed.

After Anger Passes: Emotions and Thoughts

After anger has settled, we can be left with a lot of other feelings and thoughts, like after-shocks following an earthquake. If we broke something, we may feel ashamed. If we screamed at someone we love, we may feel sorry. The aftershocks of anger can leave us with difficult thoughts about ourselves. Feeling helpless may make us think, "What can I do?" Feeling guilty may come with the thought, "I am not being a good person."

It is important to get to know some of the feelings and thoughts we have after anger has settled so we can choose different ways of acting in the future.

Below are some feelings you may have after anger has settled:

- **Ashamed:** "I'm not being a good person."
- **Embarrassed:** "I wish people hadn't seen me act that way!"
- **Guilty:** "I feel so bad for saying that."
- **Helpless:** "I don't know what to do when I'm angry."
- **Relieved:** "Whew! I'm glad that's over."
- **Scared:** "I hope Mom and Dad will forgive me."

Circle the feelings you have felt before. You may have had other thoughts or feelings that come as an aftershock of anger. If you have, list them below.

- -

- -

- -

- -

- -

After Anger Passes: Effects on Others

Everything we do and say affects those around us, even our pets. If you have a pet, have you ever noticed how he or she acts when someone in the house is angry? Dogs may bark more. Cats may run and hide.

Anger is a powerful force that makes people scared about what may happen if it gets out of control. When we experience another person's anger, we tend to remember that moment better than less intense times in our lives. This is because our brain tries to remember potentially dangerous situations, people, and places. That way, we can avoid them or know how to deal with them in the future.

Think of a time you were around someone who was angry. Draw a picture of what was happening.

What did you feel in your body? -

- -

What did you think about this person? -

- -

What did you have the urge or instinct to do then? What would you like to do in the future?

- -

- -

Talk to an adult who is close to you and ask them to share a story about a time you were angry. It may be difficult to hear what they say, but remember that it will help you understand the effects of your anger so you can choose a better way in the future.

INTERVIEW QUESTIONS

How did you feel when I became angry? -

- -

What were your instincts and urges when you saw how angry I was? -

- -

WHAT ELSE CAN ANGER BE?

Our feelings have different intensities. Like the volume on a phone, some of our feelings are quieter and some are louder. When we unpack our feelings, we can see that many can be within us at the same time. Having so many feelings at once can be confusing, but when we look at them one at a time, we feel more in control and able to give ourselves what we need to feel calmer.

Anger is a loud feeling that can sometimes drown out quieter feelings. Sometimes you feel the loudness of anger but not any of the quieter feelings that may have come before anger began to roar. For example, you may feel worried about the first day of school. When someone tells you that you must go anyway, the worries that you may not make friends or have a nice teacher can quickly turn into the roar of anger. You may also feel a quieter sadness because a friend has to move far away, and you won't get to see them as often. Before you know it, you feel very angry, screaming, "It's not fair!" as your friend drives away.

Quieter feelings like worry and sadness can be easy to miss. They may start as a feeling in the pit of your stomach or a fluttering of your heartbeat. You may even notice an urge to cry or be hugged. When we catch the quieter feelings before they get louder, we are better able to ask for what we need and help ourselves with kindness and understanding.

The following activities will help you get to know the quieter feelings that come before or with anger.

Getting to Know Fear

When we are fearful or worried, it is usually because something new is about to happen or something important to us may be taken away. We may feel afraid when people close to us argue or when we try to make new friends. Fear can make the heart beat faster and make us want to be around someone we feel safe with. It can make us want to stay home instead of doing things that are good for us, things that help us become brave and confident. When we see our fear clearly, we can let people close to us know and ask for their help and kindness.

Close your eyes and ask yourself, "When do I get scared?" Some memories of times you were scared may come to mind. Write what you discover below.

When do I feel afraid? _

_ _

What worries me? _

_ _

Now close your eyes again and see if you can remember a time recently when you were fearful. See if you can notice how fear feels in your body. You can consider different parts of the body and how they feel.

How do your head, face, and neck feel? _

What do you feel in your chest, hands, and belly? _

How do your legs and feet feel? _

_ _

_ _

Draw how worry feels in your body, using shapes and colors that capture how fear feels.

Getting to Know Sadness

Sadness can be a difficult feeling. We may feel sad when something fun comes to an end or when someone says something hurtful. Sadness can come up when we lose something we care about or miss someone who lives far away. When we feel sad, we may also feel the urge to cry. When we don't feel it is safe to express our sadness, it may turn into anger. It is important to let ourselves cry and to allow sadness to visit.

Let's explore sadness so we can recognize and welcome it when it shows up next time.

First, draw a picture of what sadness looks like to you.

Then draw a picture of what you look like when you are sad.

Describe a time you felt sad recently.

What did you do when you felt sad?

What clues did your body give you that you were sad?

Getting to Know Disappointment

We feel disappointment when we are let down. We may be let down when a friend cancels sleepover plans or when we don't get what we want. We all feel disappointed at times because there are so many things we can't control. Plans get changed, people change their minds, and sometimes things don't work as they're supposed to.

When we let ourselves feel disappointment, it can move through us like a wave, allowing us to bounce back after it's gone and find something enjoyable to look forward to.

Draw a picture of a time you were disappointed.

What does disappointment feel like in your body?

What other feelings did you have when you were disappointed?

PART TWO

What Happens When I Feel Angry?

What We'll Learn

Anger can be like quicksand. We can be happy, doing well, then all of a sudden fall into a feeling that can be hard to get out of.

Many situations and interactions with people can make us feel angry. In our great big world, all of us are trying to be happy and get along as best we can. Sometimes what we want doesn't match up with what someone else wants, and we have to do things we don't really want to do. This can make us feel frustrated, annoyed, and angry.

Part 1 introduced us to anger by exploring what it feels like and when it comes up. Now, we'll look more deeply at the causes of anger, what we do when we feel angry, and the effects of our anger. We'll see that sometimes anger can be caused by feelings from within us, like hunger and tiredness. We'll also explore how anger can be caused by events outside us, like playing a game with someone who cheats, or needing to stop an activity while you're still having fun. We will get to know how our anger can affect other people, and we will consider how anger gets in the way of getting what we really want.

There will always be pockets of quicksand in our lives, but we can learn to spot them in time and step around them so we don't fall in.

WHAT MAKES ME FEEL ANGRY?

Does anger seem to strike when you least expect it? Do you ever feel confused about why some people get angry very easily?

Not all people get angry at the same things. The way we live and the things we are taught affect our anger habits.

We can't control what other people say and do. Some people will be kind and sensitive. Others will be unkind and insensitive. Sometimes we have to go places we don't want to go (like the dentist) or do things we don't like to do (like wait in line).

Even though we wish we didn't have to go to certain places or do certain things, when we learn to recognize these things as causes of our annoyance, frustration, and anger, we can use our creativity to choose new actions.

Our body gives us clues that we may become angry soon. Getting annoyed or cranky is our body's way of telling us we should take care of a need we have. For example, we may get irritated or angry when we are hungry or tired. If we give our body food or sleep when we need it, we will feel happier and more in control.

When causes of anger don't come from within us, they come from interactions or events outside us. For example, a lot can happen when you play a game. You may feel competitive and want to win. You may want to play fair so you know you are winning because of your efforts and strategies. If you play with someone who cheats during the game, you could feel angry because they decided winning is more important than playing fairly.

We can also get angry when we feel stuck in a situation that is difficult to get out of. For example, you may feel uncomfortable or stressed during a certain part of the school day. However, you can't leave the class without getting in trouble, so you feel stuck, which can trigger anger.

Getting to know the causes of our anger helps us be prepared, so when it happens we can be kinder and more patient with ourselves and others.

Anger also has different speeds and intensities. Like spiciness in food, some spice gives us a short jolt and fades away quickly, while stronger spices leave our whole mouth feeling hot even after we drink something to wash the taste away.

The next activity will help us see which people and events cause more or less intense anger in us. It will help us be prepared for those extra-spicy moments.

Clues from Within

Sometimes, if our bodies don't feel well, we are more likely to get angry. Anger lets us know we don't like what's going on inside, or we need something to feel better.

For example, it can be hard to keep our cool when we are hungry, tired, bored, sick, or lonely. If we can notice the body clues when they start, we can stop anger from getting out of control.

Choose one of those feelings (hungry, tired, bored, sick, or lonely) and draw a picture of how it feels in your body. Then, write what that feeling would say if it could speak.

Now close your eyes and think about a time you felt the way you did in your drawing. Write about that time.

How about when you feel other difficult feelings? Think of some ways you can help yourself.

I feel bored when _____

_____ .

What is something I can do when I feel bored? _____

Clues from Within, *continued*

I feel lonely when _____

_____ .

What are three things I can do when I feel lonely?

1. _____

2. _____

3. _____

I am hungriest at (name time of day) _____

_____ .

Some things I can do to take care of my hunger are:

1. _____

2. _____

3. _____

Clues from Outside

So many things can make us angry. We may feel angry when we cannot control people or situations, or when family members or friends say or do something we do not like.

Most people get angry for many of the same reasons. For example, we tend to get angry when we feel physically threatened, when we are insulted, when we feel protective of our friends or family, or when rules are broken.

Remembering the moments that can cause us anger will help us be better prepared for them and know better ways of handling them.

Close your eyes and imagine a time when you were angry. What happened right before, during, and after?

Before _____

_____

_____

During _____

_____

_____

After _____

_____

_____

Clues from Outside, *continued*

See if you can write down three more times you felt angry. You can choose from the list or think of some on your own.

1. _____

2. _____

3. _____

- Being stuck in a class you don't like
- Someone breaking the rules
- Someone calling you names
- Someone putting down your friend or family
- Someone stopping you from playing
- Someone taking your belongings away
- Someone threatening to hurt you

Take a few minutes to think about the people, places, and events that trigger anger and list them below. You may want to ask an adult to help you remember times when you got angry, so you can add them to your list.

PEOPLE	PLACES	EVENTS

Rating Intensity

Each upsetting event leaves us with different levels of anger, depending on how much something bothers us. As we get more and more angry, we feel like we have less and less control over how we feel, what we say, and what we do.

As you think about the events, people, and feelings that make you angry, see if you can rate how strong the anger is.

1. Feeling calm, friendly, and in control
2. Feeling a little annoyed or bothered but still in control
3. Feeling hurt or amped up—noticing you are getting warmer or your heart is beating faster or getting warmer
4. Feeling a lot of energy in your body—getting the urge to hit or run or feeling you have very little control left
5. Feeling furious—noticing an urge to scream or break something

Below, rate each event, person, or feeling using the anger scale of 1 to 5, with 1 being the lowest.

Seeing someone cheat during a game   - - - - - - - - - -

Hearing someone call your friend "dumb"   - - - - - - - - - -

Feeling really tired and hungry after school   - - - - - - - - - -

Mom or Dad telling you it's time to stop playing video games   - - - - - - - - - -

Someone telling you that your clothes are ugly   - - - - - - - - - -

Feeling stuck in a class you don't like   - - - - - - - - - -

Mom or Dad saying you have to go visit a relative you don't like   - - - - - - - - - -

Feeling lonely and having nothing to do   - - - - - - - - - -

Someone playing a trick on you   - - - - - - - - - -

Now, think of an inside cause of anger (like feeling tired or hungry) and an outside cause of anger (like name-calling or having something taken away from you) you have experienced. Rate the intensity of the anger.

Inside cause _____ Rating _____

Outside cause _____ Rating _____

INTERNAL

EXTERNAL

WHO MAKES ME FEEL ANGRY?

Think about all the people in your life. There are people you see almost every day, like your family members, friends, and teachers and helpers at school. There are also important people whom you see less often, like relatives and friends who live far away.

We always want to get along with the people closest to us. We want them to be happy, peaceful, healthy, and safe. However, when our anger gets out of control, we may say hurtful or scary things that cause those we care about to feel afraid, angry, or distant from us.

There are also people who may be difficult to be around. Perhaps they act inconsiderately or say things that hurt our feelings. These may be people we would rather not be around, but who are in our lives because they are part of our family or in our school. We may feel okay being mean back to them because their actions make us feel hurt or angry. However, later on, we often see that being mean or angry does not help us get along.

Knowing What We Feel, Knowing What to Say

Difficult feelings often come up when we want something we are not getting. For example, when someone interrupts us a lot, we may *feel* annoyed because we *want* cooperation and attention.

If a little brother or sister is taking your toys without asking, you may *feel* angry because you *want* your things to be in order. You may also *want* support from your parents to help your sibling understand this.

Learning to name your feelings and wants can take some practice. It is helpful for you and your family members, though, because when you can clearly identify your feelings, you can communicate them to others and get the help you need to make things work better.

With the help of an adult, think of three events that brought up a difficult feeling. They don't have to be big events. They can be small annoyances you got over quickly. If you like, ask an adult to share some of their difficult moments, too. You'll see that it happens to all of us!

Then see if you can name the feeling you felt. You can use the feelings list or think of your own feeling words. Write down what you think you needed to make you feel better. You can choose from the wants and needs list or come up with your own.

FEELINGS LIST

- Annoyed
- Frustrated
- Grumpy
- Helpless
- Impatient
- Irritated
- Sad
- Scared
- Worried

WANTS AND NEEDS LIST

- A hug or cuddle
- Being included
- Cooperation
- Encouragement
- Food/water
- Free time
- Freedom to choose
- Reassurance
- Sleep
- Understanding

Knowing What We Feel, Knowing What to Say, *continued*

WHAT HAPPENED?	WHAT DID YOU FEEL?	WHAT DID YOU WANT OR NEED?
1.		
2.		
3.		

When Things Get Hard at Home

Some people live with a lot of family members. Some live with very few. Some see aunts, uncles, and cousins often. Others don't.

Although we usually love our family very much, some of our family members may be harder to be around than others. Maybe you have a grumpy aunt or an annoying little brother who brings up difficult feelings such as sadness, frustration, or confusion.

Many of these difficult people also have very nice parts. They may just be harder to see. It helps to think about what the person does that makes them difficult to be around, so we can name the problem when it comes up. This will help us better understand what makes us upset and clear up any confusion about that person.

Being in relationships with people is like a chemistry experiment. Like chemicals, some explode when they are mixed, and others blend well. When we understand the chemical reaction that takes place when we are with someone we feel angry around, we can be more prepared to handle our anger with care.

FAMILY MEMBERS

- Mom
- Dad
- Stepmom/Stepdad
- Brothers/Sisters
- Aunt
- Uncle
- Cousins
- Grandma
- Grandpa

This is a list of just *some* family members who may be in your life. You may see other relatives, such as great-grandmas or great-grandpas, often and want to include them, too.

When Things Get Hard at Home, *continued*

As you think about your family and look at the list, which people are difficult for you to be around sometimes?

What difficult things happen when you are around them? This could be a feeling you get, the way you talk to each other, or maybe the way you act together.

These are some sticky situations that may happen:

- Being interrupted
- Being teased
- Playing together
- Sharing with someone
- Someone being very strict

Now, choose one or two difficult people and fill out the chart. How do you feel around them or after you are with them? What do you need from them to feel better? Take a look at the example to give you an idea of what to write.

WHO IS THE PERSON?	WHAT HAPPENS?	HOW DO YOU FEEL AFTER?	WHAT DO YOU NEED TO HELP YOU FEEL BETTER?
Jay	He tells me what to do.	Angry	I need him to ask me instead of telling me to do things.

Conflicts at School

School is a big part of our lives. We spend six or seven hours there every weekday, which means we become very familiar with our classmates, teachers, and other adults there.

People at school can be hard to get along with for different reasons. You may have a teacher who is strict, or a classmate who is distracting in class. You may see other children treated unfairly, or you may be treated unfairly yourself.

Let's take what we learned in the previous activity and apply it to the people at school.

Think of two or three people who are difficult to get along with at school. Then write down what's difficult about them. Finally, think back to the list of needs from Activity 1 in this section. Write down some things you may need.

Here is an example to follow.

PERSON	WHAT'S DIFFICULT?	WHAT DO YOU NEED?
Sara	She gets distracted when I am talking to her.	Attention and understanding

What We Have in Common

We all have a lot more in common than we think. Even though people can be difficult, they also have a lot of likeable parts we may have trouble seeing.

Let's think of a few difficult people, either at home or school. Think about what we have in common with them.

In the list are some enjoyable qualities that people can have. You can use this list for the questions that follow or think of words of your own to describe what you like about the people.

- Caring
- Creative
- Friendly
- Funny
- Generous
- Gets over things quickly

- Good listener
- Helpful
- Includes others
- Playful
- Smart
- Supportive

Who is someone you find easy to like or love? What about them is easy to like?

I like/love _____ .

I like _____ about him/her.

Who is someone you find easy to like some of the time? What is easy to like and what is hard to like?

Sometimes, I like _____ .

It's easy to like him/her when _____ .

It's hard to like him/her when _____ .

What We Have in Common, *continued*

Who is someone you find difficult to get along with? What is hard to like? What do you have in common with them?

It's difficult to like _ .

He/she is hard to like because _ .

I have _ , _ ,

and _ in common with him/her.

How does it feel to think of things you have in common with this difficult person?

_ _

What is hard to like about yourself sometimes? What is easy to love about yourself?

It's hard to like myself when _ .

I am lovable because _ .

HOW DO I SHOW MY ANGER?

The ways we show anger are affected by our personalities and habits at home and school. Some people may yell a lot when they feel angry. Others may quietly stew like a pot of boiling water. Getting to know your personal anger style will help you begin to make changes.

In the first activity in this section, you can think about how you show anger when certain events happen at home and at school. In the second activity, we will look at the differences between healthy and unhealthy ways of dealing with our anger.

Healthy ways of dealing with anger require a little bit of *holding back* from what we usually do. Healthy actions include going for a walk or taking some deep breaths before we say or do anything hurtful or scary. Just like learning a musical instrument or playing a sport takes practice and determination, learning healthy ways of dealing with anger takes time and practice.

The third activity invites you to be creative and think of little changes you can make to prepare for challenging times. Thinking and planning ahead can help prevent feelings like boredom and frustration from appearing and leading to anger.

How Does My Anger Take Charge?

Many stressful events throughout the day can make us feel angry very quickly. Read the stressful events below and write in what your usual response would be to each. Add in a few examples of your own.

STRESSFUL EVENTS: MY RESPONSE

A parent says, "No, you can't watch more TV." → _____

_____

You get a bad grade in school. → _____

_____

You have five minutes left on a test and you feel confused. → _____

_____

A friend cancels a sleepover. → _____

_____

Your sibling takes one of your toys and won't give it back. → _____

_____ → _____

_____ → _____

As you look back at your responses, do you notice any that happen often? Write below about some of the habits you noticed.

HABITS WHEN I AM UPSET

Expressing Anger: Is It Helpful or Unhelpful?

When we feel angry, it is easy to say and do things we feel bad about later, when our anger has settled.

The chart will help you remember some unhelpful things you tend to do when you feel angry. It will also help you think of some helpful ways of letting your anger settle.

UNHELPFUL RESPONSE TO ANGER	HELPFUL RESPONSE TO ANGER
Name-calling	Do mindful belly breathing
Physically hurting someone	Go for a walk or run
Saying "I hate you"	Say "I am angry and I need help"
Screaming	Squeeze a stress ball
Slamming doors	Write down what you are mad about
Throwing things	

As you think about times you get angry, write down some unhelpful and helpful ways you have handled your anger. For example, do you remember a time you walked away to cool down or went to be by yourself for a while before yelling? Ask an adult to help you think of times when you or they were angry, and add the examples to your list.

UNHELPFUL RESPONSE TO ANGER	HELPFUL RESPONSE TO ANGER

On the Lookout

Even though there are many things we have to do, like go to school, sit in a car, brush our teeth, and go to sleep, we can find creative ways to make them less frustrating and more enjoyable. When we know we are about to do something that may make us angry, we can use calming and reframing tools to look at the situation in a different way.

For example, some people feel annoyed and frustrated when they have to wait in line at a store. If you are one of those people and you know you will be going to a store and may start to feel bored or impatient, you can have a couple of ideas handy to help you with those feelings.

Some things you could do include using your five senses (sight, hearing, taste, smell, and touch) to notice things you never noticed before in the store, playing a game with your mom or dad, or looking for ways to be helpful with shopping or other errands.

When we know something that makes us angry is coming up, being prepared for it helps us feel calm and flexible.

Let's think of some events that make us angry and write down new ways of handling the situation.

For example, you may know you get angry with a friend or family member who doesn't take care of your things. You get angry when they come over because they want to play with your toys and won't take no for an answer.

Can you think of something helpful you can do? _

_ _

Some suggestions:
1. Find an activity you can both do together, like playing a sport, cooking, or making crafts.
2. Ask a parent or another adult to help you put some of your favorite toys away so they are safe.

Think about something that made you feel angry recently. What was it? _

_ _

_ _

What are some things you can change about the situation, so you are less likely to get angry?

_____

_____

What are some things you can think about to help you feel calmer in this situation? _ _ _ _ _ _ _ _ _ _

_____

_____

How could you handle this situation differently? _

_____

_____

What's something comforting you could do? _

_____

_____

WHEN I GIVE ANGER, WHAT DO I GET BACK?

Feelings can be contagious and can spread like a cold. Pleasant feelings such as happiness, excitement, and calm can spread just as easily as anger and frustration. When we are around happy people, we tend to feel happier, and when we are around grumpy people, we can feel grumpy, too.

In one of the following activities, you will practice role-playing by putting yourself in someone else's shoes and imagining you are on the receiving end of anger. Understanding how your anger affects others builds *empathy*. Empathy is our ability to imagine how someone else feels, so we can offer care and kindness to them.

Sometimes, when we are in the heat of anger, we forget to think about how our anger affects other people. When we are calm, it is much easier to reflect on how anger gets in the way of getting what we want and how anger can hurt the people we care about.

In the following activities, we'll explore the ways we express anger. We'll think of new responses to anger that we can choose instead of our automatic reactions that may be hurtful. This will help us show kindness to ourselves and others.

How Anger Affects Others

Every time someone makes us angry, a reaction happens inside us. This can be a thought, feeling, or body sensation that leads us to do or say something. Whatever we do or say to that person has consequences that are pleasant (we like them), unpleasant (we don't like them), or neutral (they're okay, or we're not sure how we feel about them).

The order looks something like this:

Upsetting Event → **Thought/Feeling** → **Reaction** → **Consequences**

Think about times when you get angry at someone. Then look at the example in the chart and fill in three interactions of your own.

EVENT	THOUGHT/ FEELING	REACTION	CONSEQUENCES
Mom tells me to stop playing video games.	"I'm not ready to stop."	Say, "No! I'm still playing and I'll play for as long as I want."	Mom gets angry and unplugs the TV.

How Anger Affects Others, *continued*

Choose two examples from the chart and think of a response that could be kinder and more pleasant for the person you care about.

Event: _

Kinder response: _

_ _

_ _

Event: _

Kinder response: _

_ _

_ _

Building Empathy

For this activity, you will need an adult to role-play with. You will act as a family member or friend who sometimes receives your anger. This will help you understand what it feels like when you are around someone who has lost control of their anger.

   Look at the previous activity and pick an interaction you wrote about. You are going to play the role of your parent, sibling, or friend, while the adult pretends to be you. For example, you'll say what your mom or dad says when they ask you to stop playing video games or announce it is time for bed. Then the adult will act out your reaction, the way they see it. Continue talking back and forth until you've acted out the whole situation. When you are done, answer the following questions.

What event did you choose? _____

What feelings came up during the role-play? _____

_____

What did you think about as you watched the adult act like you? _____

_____

Now that you understand another person's point of view better, how might you act differently next time?

_____

_____

Needs that Help

We all need certain things that help us get along with each other. In every relationship, we give and we receive. We may be good at giving certain things, like attention to a friend who wants to talk, or kindness when a friend is upset. Other things like patience and consideration may be harder for us to give, especially when we are not feeling our best.

In this activity, you will explore three things we need to give to others and receive back from them: cooperation, understanding, and reassurance. They help prevent anger and help us when we are already upset. Read about each one and then think about times you needed them.

Cooperation means people work together to make something happen. You cooperate when you share the responsibility of a school project or work as a family to clean the house.

Write about a time you wanted cooperation but didn't get it. _

_ _

_ _

When we receive *understanding*, we know and trust that someone can relate to how we feel and why. They are not judging us as good or bad. They are simply trying to make sense of our feelings and actions.

Write about a time you felt judged instead of understood. _

_ _

_ _

How can you help people understand you better? _

_ _

_ _

When someone offers us *reassurance*, they are telling us that everything will work out, that things will be okay, and we will feel better again soon. We may need reassurance if we are sad or if something fun is ending and we are frustrated.

Think about a time you were disappointed and write about it. _

_ _

_ _

What are some words of reassurance that would have helped you feel better at that time? Think about what you could say to a friend who was disappointed.

_ _

_ _

_ _

HOW IS MY ANGER WORKING FOR ME?

Anger, like most difficult emotions, usually comes up because we want something and are not getting it. If we feel angry because we've struck out at a baseball game, it's probably because we wanted to hit the ball and let our team know we are a valuable player. When we get cranky during a long road trip, it may be because we want to be outside and stretch our legs.

Although anger can be a natural reaction to a lot of unpleasant events, it often leaves us feeling alone and disconnected from those who can compromise with us, encourage us, and help us get what we want.

The first step in getting what we want in difficult situations is to understand how our actions can make things worse. This starts with identifying our unhelpful words and actions, like name-calling and door-slamming. As we think about times we have acted this way, we can understand why we didn't get what we wanted.

Once we understand our unhealthy, angry actions, we can think about better ways of handling our anger. When you are in the heat of anger, it can be hard to choose a healthy action. Thinking of better, healthy actions when you are calm will help you remember the healthy actions the next time you feel angry. Helpful responses usually involve some holding back or stepping away to get some space from the thing causing our anger.

However, sometimes, if we are in a classroom or a car for example, we can't walk away. At times like that, it is important to pause *inside* ourselves. This can feel like pressing on the brakes in your mind, so you don't say or do what first comes to mind. Holding back gives us some space between our feelings and urges and what we decide to do with them, so we can *choose* instead of *react*. If we learn to do this, we're more likely to get the things we want, even in a difficult situation.

Who's in the Driver's Seat?

Anger can change the way we see people and situations. It is helpful to recognize the signs that tell you whether you are seeing things from your calm mind or your angry mind. When you know the signs, you can consider how acting from your calm mind helps you get what you want and keeps your relationships with others healthy.

Calm mind can do this:

- **Imagine the consequences:** "How would he feel if I grabbed the ball away?"
- **See different sides of a situation:** "Maybe it was an accident instead of on purpose."
- **Be understanding:** "Maybe she's having a bad day."
- **Hold back or walk away:** "I need to calm my mind before saying or doing anything."
- **See different feelings clearly:** "I feel angry, disappointed, and sad."

Angry mind is like this:

- **Reactive:** "I'll do what I want."
- **Does what it wants when it wants to:** "They deserve to be hurt because they hurt me."

Write an example of a time you got angry: _

_ _

What did you do? _

_ _

Were you in your angry mind or calm mind? _

_ _

What were the consequences? _

_ _

Who's in the Driver's Seat?, *continued*

Write a few examples of what your angry mind says and what your calm mind says when things are difficult.

ANGRY MIND	CALM MIND
They deserve it!	I want to be mean, but I am taking a breath instead.
I hate them!	I am very mad, but my anger won't last forever.

How do people respond when you act or speak from your calm mind instead of your angry mind?

What Could I Do Instead?

Anger can move so fast sometimes it can feel like a speeding train. The speed and strength of anger can make us do things (like hitting) or say things (like name-calling) that we feel sorry for later. However, we can find ways of slowing the anger train down so we make sure we keep ourselves and others safe.

Can you remember a time when you were so angry a friend or family member didn't feel safe around you? By thinking about different ways of responding to anger, you can make sure you are taking care of your anger in healthier ways, ways you can feel good about later. When you do this, you're more likely to end up in a good place at the end of a tough situation.

Match each triggering event to a healthy action you could take. Add a few examples of your own in the space provided.

TRIGGERING EVENTS

- Being told it's time to go to bed
- Being told it's time to stop playing video games or watching TV
- Having to eat something you don't want to eat
- Having to go to school when you don't want to
- Having to share your toys
- Hearing "No" when you ask for something you want at the store
- Losing a baseball game
- Waiting in line

- -

- -

- -

HEALTHY ACTIONS

- Imagine something you have that you really like
- Remember that anger will fade away and not last forever
- Say how you feel using "I feel . . ."
- Take a shower or bath
- Take a walk nearby
- Take three deep breaths with your eyes closed

- -

- -

- -

- -

- -

Changing Our Tone Changes the Tune

When we feel angry, the tone of our voice changes. Sometimes our voice gets louder or sounds aggressive. Our parents, friends, and loved ones can hear the small changes in tone and start to feel nervous or get ready to defend themselves against an attack from anger.

Defenses are like walls that people build to protect themselves. When the walls go up, it is harder to cooperate. As we've discovered, anger bubbles up in us because we need something we are not getting. Being aware of the way we ask for what we want and the tone of our voice when asking increases the chance that people will cooperate with us. This takes some self-control, so it may not be easy at first. However, as you practice more and more, it will become more natural to pause before speaking and acting out of anger.

Think back to some of the things you needed when you were angry. For example, sometimes we need more free time before starting homework, or something to look forward to when we are disappointed.

Changing Our Tone Changes the Tune, *continued*

Draw a picture of a way of asking or acting on your anger that would not get you what you wanted.

Now draw a picture that shows you getting what you want by speaking or acting in a calmer way.

What Should I Do With My Anger?

What We'll Learn

In this part of the workbook, you will learn many new ways of greeting your anger and other big feelings with kindness and paying attention to your feelings. You will learn what it means to *host* your difficult feelings, like you would welcome a visitor to your home.

Our brain tends to focus on things that could be dangerous, scary, or make us angry, but we can balance that out with fun and easy exercises that help us pay attention to everything good in our lives.

There are many ways to take care of ourselves by being kind, patient, and thankful. You will see you have a lot more control over your feelings than you imagine. As you discover what to do with anger, you will also learn healthy ways of telling people how you feel and what you need. You will discover ways of understanding how others feel and what they need when they feel angry, too.

In the last section, you will spend time thinking and writing about what makes you and others happy. As you complete the last section of this book, you'll see you do have control and can choose what to do the next time anger comes to visit.

WHO CAN I BE IF I'M NOT ANGRY ME?

Now that we have learned more about what makes us angry and what can happen when we are angry, let's explore what to do to feel calmer and more in control.

One of the most helpful tools we can learn is *mindfulness*. Being mindful means paying attention to the present moment, to whatever is happening, with kindness and acceptance. We often try to get rid of things we don't like and want more of what we do like. This is normal and natural. But we can also be patient with ourselves and welcome difficulties as though they are visitors stopping by. The things we pay attention to include our five senses—what we see, smell, taste, touch, and hear. They also include the sensations in our bodies, our thoughts and feelings, and our relationships with other people. We pay attention to these different parts of life all the time. However, we often don't know where our attention is or how to control it.

One way to think of your attention is to imagine it as a flashlight you shine on certain things—you choose where to shine the light. To train our inner flashlight—our attention—we need to practice a little bit every day. One way to practice is to anchor our attention to our breath, our body, or sounds around us. Just like an anchor keeps a boat from drifting too far out to sea, the anchor for our attention lets us know when our attention has drifted, so we can bring it back.

It is also important to know and practice ways of calming our body. When we relax the muscles in the body, the mind relaxes, too. You will learn how to tense your muscles on purpose and then release them. That will let you feel the relaxation you created in your body and mind.

There are so many creative ways of calming ourselves down when we feel angry. You may enjoy a warm bath or some alone time in your bed. We'll explore some activities that help settle your anger and allow you to speak and act from your calm self.

When we feel angry, it is difficult to talk to people clearly and with consideration. So, we will practice some ways of telling people what we need when we are upset. Practice will make it easier when anger is present.

Brake, Breathe, See, Choose

The first thing to do when you feel angry is to *brake* or stop what you are doing or about to do. Then take a deep breath, feeling your belly go out and in when you inhale and exhale. Then pay attention to the anger clues in your body. Notice sensations such as heat, tingling, pressure, and tightness. When you feel a bit calmer, choose an action that is considerate and helpful to you and the person you are with.

This activity gives you two ways to calm yourself when you feel angry, so you'll be able to make choices from your calm mind.

GETTING TO KNOW YOUR BREATH

Close your eyes and take two deep breaths in and out through your nose. Pay attention to your belly moving. Then close your eyes and take two deep breaths, noticing your chest moving up and down. Finally, take three normal breaths through your nose. Pay attention to the air as it moves in and out through your nose. Try counting your breaths silently, noticing the feeling of your belly moving as you breathe. As you breathe in, count *1, 1, 1*. And as you breathe out, count *1, 1, 1*. Keep counting all the way up to *4* like this and then start again.

Where is it easiest to notice your breath? _____

What sensations do you notice in that area? _____

It is important to take time each day to anchor your attention to your breathing. This helps your prefrontal cortex learn to help your amygdala when you start to feel angry. You can set a timer for one to five minutes and practice anchoring to your breath.

SQUEEZE AND LET GO

Did you know that your muscles get tighter when you feel angry or frustrated? Sometimes releasing the tightness can help us feel more relaxed and in control of our feelings.

In this exercise, we practice squeezing and releasing different parts of the body. Then we can see how it changes how our mind feels.

Start by sitting down and getting comfortable.

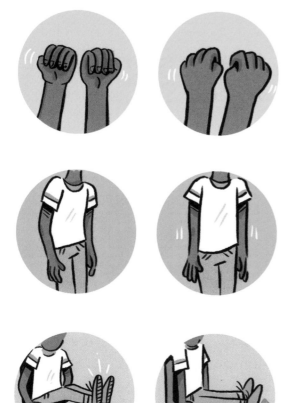

Hands: Make fists with your hands, tucking your thumbs under your fingers. Squeeze your fists, imagining all your frustration being pulled into your hands from your body like a magnet. Count to 10 slowly while you hold the squeeze. Then take a deep breath in through your nose. As you breathe out, release and stretch out your hands. Imagine frustration leaving your body as you release your hands.

Arms: Bend your elbows and squeeze your arms into the sides of your body. Count to 10 and then take a deep breath and release your arms as you breathe out.

Legs: Sit back in your chair and lift your feet from the floor as you straighten your legs out. Feel your leg muscles working and your knees pressing together. Count to 10 and then take a deep breath in and out as you slowly lower your feet to the ground.

Now close your eyes, take a deep breath, and notice how your body and mind feel.

My body feels _____

_____ .

My mind feels _____

_____ .

Making Friends with My Five Senses

When we get angry, we get tunnel vision. That means it is hard to see what's going on around us. When we pause to notice our five senses, one at a time, we bring ourselves back to the present moment.

As you look around you right now, see if you can spot five things you haven't noticed before. Write them down.

1. _____

2. _____

3. _____

4. _____

5. _____

Bonus: Play "I Spy" with family members while you're walking or waiting in line.

Now, set a timer for one minute and close your eyes. Listen for how many different sounds you can hear. When you are done, draw or write down the sounds you heard.

You can continue to notice your other senses—taste, smell, and touch—when you are calm or starting to feel angry. Next time you are close to nature, close your eyes and take a deep breath. Notice what scents are in the air. Next time you take a bite of food, close your eyes and notice how the food tastes, what it feels like on your tongue, and anything else you can about what you're eating.

What Can I Do Instead?

Different situations require different behaviors. At school, our teachers expect us to pay attention and ask when we need things, like a restroom break. At home, we have more freedom to do what we like when we want.

In the following activity, we'll match different situations to appropriate responses so we're prepared when they happen. There can be more than one right answer for each situation. Just choose one you think would be most helpful to you, and draw a line from the situation to your response.

SITUATION	YOUR RESPONSE
Feeling disappointed after plans are cancelled	Asking for a hug
Feeling sad or angry because of something someone says	Asking to go to the restroom
Feeling threatened by someone at school	Asking to take a walk
Getting a bad grade on a test	Being with a pet
Seeing someone cheat during a game	Counting your breaths
Someone teasing you	Going to the restroom for privacy
When Mom or Dad says it's time to stop playing video games or watching TV	Listening to music
When you have to go somewhere you don't want to go, like the dentist or a relative's house	Reading a story
When your brother or sister breaks something of yours	Squeezing your hands and letting go
	Taking a bath or shower
	Telling a friend you need to be alone for a little while
	Watching a movie
	Watching things outside in nature
	Writing a note to the teacher asking for a small break from participation until you are calmer

Rating My New Behaviors

Some new behaviors will be easier than others, but the ones that are harder will get easier over time as you practice them.

As you read the list of new behaviors, take a few moments to think about how easy or difficult they are for you to practice. You can use numbers 1 to 5 to rate how hard they are, with 1 being super easy and 5 being very difficult.

_ _ _ _ _ _ **Asking for a hug**

_ _ _ _ _ _ **Asking to go to the restroom**

_ _ _ _ _ _ **Asking to take a walk**

_ _ _ _ _ _ **Being with a pet**

_ _ _ _ _ _ **Counting your breaths**

_ _ _ _ _ _ **Going to the restroom for privacy**

_ _ _ _ _ _ **Listening to music**

_ _ _ _ _ _ **Reading a story**

_ _ _ _ _ _ **Squeezing your fists and letting go**

_ _ _ _ _ _ **Taking a bath or shower**

_ _ _ _ _ _ **Telling a friend you need to be alone for a little while**

_ _ _ _ _ _ **Watching a movie**

_ _ _ _ _ _ **Watching things outside in nature**

_ _ _ _ _ _ **Writing a note to the teacher asking for a small break from participation until you are calmer**

Which one of the above behaviors do you want to try out this week?

- -

How Do I Ask for What I Need?

It can be difficult to ask for help when we feel angry. There are appropriate ways to ask for a break when it is especially difficult to calm ourselves. Let's look at some ways we can ask for what we need when we are not able to calm ourselves right away.

Fill in the blanks, imagining how you might ask for a break. Then match the requests to the people you might ask.

- Babysitter
- Coach
- Friend
- Parent
- Teacher

I'm feeling _____

and I need to _____ .

It's hard to talk right now. Can I _____

_____ **and then we can talk later?**

I feel _____

_____ **and don't really know what I need. Can you help me figure it out?**

I can't _____ right now.

Can I _____ ?

I really need to _____

because I feel _____ .

WHAT DO I NEED WHEN I FEEL ANGRY?

In the heat of anger, figuring out what we need can leave us feeling confused. This is because there are so many fast-moving thoughts and feelings swirling around that it is hard to see things clearly.

In the next three activities, you will use your imagination to consider the things, people, and places that help you feel calm, safe, and comfortable.

After an angry outburst, it is easy to be hard on ourselves. We often feel guilty or ashamed of something we said or did when we were angry. We also think that if we are not hard on ourselves, we may act unwisely again in the future.

However, that's when we need kindness more than ever. Our feelings are like crying babies who need loving attention and care.

Just imagine a friend who felt angry or sad. What helped them feel better? Often, we find it easy to be kind and supportive to our friends when they feel hurt. We can turn this same kindness back on ourselves.

When anger strikes, think about what you need to feel better, like kindness or forgiveness, and find a way to give it to yourself.

What Do I Need to Calm Me?

Think about what makes you feel peaceful, happy, and safe. Once you know that, the next time you feel angry, you'll have ideas of what you can do to find your calm mind.

Close your eyes and ask yourself, what makes me feel peaceful? Imagine yourself doing something that makes you feel peaceful and draw it below.

What Do I Need to Calm Me?, *continued*

Now close your eyes again and ask yourself, what makes me feel calm and happy? Imagine doing something that makes you feel calm and happy and draw it below.

Lastly, close your eyes and ask yourself, what makes me feel safe? Imagine yourself feeling safe and cozy and draw a picture of it below.

Glitter Jar

Do you ever feel confused about your feelings? Do you sometimes feel like five feelings are fighting for your attention all at once? Sometimes feelings just need some extra time to be seen. When they are seen, they can start to settle on their own.

Just like the snowflakes in a snow globe, feelings get shaken up by situations, people, and events. Trying to push our feelings away or stop them is like continuing to shake the snow globe. When we do this, the feelings, like the flakes, do not get a chance to settle.

In this activity, you make your own snow globe or glitter jar, which you can use to identify your feelings and give them time to settle. Once you have identified your feelings and feel calmer, you will be able to say what you need more clearly and be able to talk about it with a calm mind.

WHAT YOU'LL NEED

- A big Mason jar
- Clear school glue
- Glitter in two or three colors

INSTRUCTIONS

1. Fill half the jar with warm water, add 2 tablespoons of glue to the water, and stir.
2. As you sprinkle the glitter into the water, think of a time you felt sad, angry, scared, and/or comforted. Share a story about a time you had one of these feelings with an adult who is helping you.
3. Add room-temperature water to fill the jar, leaving a little room at the top.
4. Seal and shake the jar.
5. Watch all of the glitter slowly float to the bottom while you notice how you feel in this moment. You may notice it's a pleasant feeling, one you like, or an unpleasant feeling, one you want to get rid of.
6. Take a deep breath and allow your feelings to be just as they are. Notice how your feelings change as the glitter floats down.

Giving Kindness to Ourselves

Sometimes we get angry at ourselves for feeling a certain way. We can feel ashamed, embarrassed, or sad when we think we have no control over our own feelings. Sometimes we forget that difficult feelings are a normal part of life everyone experiences. This can make us be even harder on ourselves and make us feel alone, like we are the only ones feeling this way.

Often, when we're angry, what we need is kindness and understanding. We can provide this to ourselves by practicing *compassion*, or the ability to see and understand our own pain or discomfort. Self-kindness and compassion remind us to take a step back and say, "Ouch! This hurts," the way we do when we bump our knee on a table. It helps us be a kind friend to ourselves and comfort ourselves the way we comfort a friend who is sad or upset.

GUIDED MEDITATION

Close your eyes and think of a recent difficult moment. As you think of this moment, put a hand over your heart and say, "Ouch!" (aloud or silently).

Think about all the other people in the world who feel this same difficult feeling. Notice how this makes you feel kindness toward them and toward yourself.

Lastly, say something kind to yourself. It could be reassuring, like "This feeling will pass soon," or loving, like "I am here and will stay with you as long as you need me to." You can also say, "May I feel peaceful. May I give my feelings room to be just as they are. May I accept my feelings and be kind to myself."

Open your eyes and notice how you feel.

What did you notice?

- -

Try these three steps the next time you feel a big, difficult feeling:

1. Put a hand over your heart and think or say, "Ouch! This is hard."
2. Think of all the people in the world who feel this, too, and feel kindness for them and yourself.
3. Say kind, reassuring words to yourself and let your feelings be just as they are.

HOW DO I TELL PEOPLE WHAT I NEED?

We use words like *sad*, *angry*, and *happy* to describe our feelings, but there are so many other words that may better explain what we really feel. For example, *restless* means it is hard for us to sit still and we have a lot of energy. *Fragile* means we feel sensitive, like we could cry easily.

Building our feeling vocabulary helps us know and share with others what we *really* feel so we can get the help we need.

When we have a difficult feeling, it is usually because there is something we need or want. It is important to be able to identify our needs so we can communicate them clearly. We may want to say, "I need *you* to stop cheating," which puts a lot of pressure on the person we say it to. Instead, we can learn to share the *pure* need: "I need cooperation and trust." This way, we can get our needs met without one person feeling all of the pressure.

After we have practiced naming our feelings and needs, it is time to make a request. A request is different from a demand. With a request, we are willing to hear no as a response. A no doesn't mean you are not going to get what you need. It just means you will have to work with someone (cooperate) to come up with ways to get what you both need.

We can only ask people to do something, because we can't *make* anyone do anything. When making a request, make it positive. Instead of telling someone what you *don't* want them to do, tell them what you *want* them to do. For example, instead of "Stop cheating," you can say, "Are you willing to play by the rules?"

Building Our Feelings Vocabulary

As you look at the list of feeling words, ask an adult to help explain words that are new to you. Then read the scenarios and write in a feeling word that describes how you might feel in that situation.

FEELING WORDS

- Bored
- Calm
- Confident
- Cranky
- Curious
- Disappointed
- Disconnected
- Embarrassed
- Excited

- Exhausted
- Fragile
- Frustrated
- Grateful
- Jealous
- Lonely
- Overwhelmed
- Panicked
- Quiet

- Refreshed
- Relaxed
- Relieved
- Restless
- Sad
- Surprised
- Worried

A close friend cancels plans last-minute. _

Someone breaks the rules of a game during recess. _ _ _ _ _ _ _ _ _ _ _ _ _ _ _ _ _ _

Someone makes fun of your clothes at school. _

You accidentally walk into the wrong classroom. _ _ _ _ _ _ _ _ _ _ _ _ _ _ _ _ _ _ _

A friend gets a new scooter that you want. _

You're waiting for Mom or Dad to get off a long phone call so you can play. _ _ _ _ _ _

You have a lot of energy and still have a two-hour drive before you arrive. _ _ _ _ _ _ _ _ _ _ _ _ _ _ _ _

All of your friends are talking about a TV show you haven't seen. _

Your mom or dad is 15 minutes late to pick you up. _

You studied hard for a test and are ready for it. _

You've had a busy day and want to rest alone. _

You haven't eaten in many hours and are very hungry. _

What Do I Really Want or Need?

Let's practice identifying what we need and communicating it by returning to some of the situations we thought about in Activity 1. Fill in the blanks by choosing a feeling and need you may have in the different situations. Ask an adult you trust to explain any words you do not know.

FEELINGS LIST

- Bored
- Calm
- Confident
- Cranky
- Curious
- Disappointed
- Disconnected
- Embarrassed
- Excited
- Exhausted
- Fragile
- Frustrated
- Grateful
- Jealous
- Lonely
- Overwhelmed
- Panicked
- Quiet
- Refreshed
- Relaxed
- Relieved
- Restless
- Sad
- Surprised
- Worried

NEEDS LIST

- Air
- Appreciation
- Attention
- Celebration
- Choice
- Connection to friends and family
- Cooperation
- Ease
- Feeling able to do something well
- Food
- Hope
- Independence
- Joy
- Love
- Movement
- Organization
- Play
- Safety
- Shelter
- Sleep
- Stability
- To be challenged
- To be understood/to understand
- To express creativity
- To express yourself
- Trust
- Water

When my friend cancelled plans, I felt _____

and I needed _____ .

When someone broke the game's rules, I felt _____

because I needed _____ .

When I was waiting for you to get off the phone, I felt _____

because I needed _____ .

When I was in the car for over two hours, I felt _____

because I needed _____ .

When you were talking about a TV show I haven't seen, I felt _____

because I needed _____ .

What Do I Really Want or Need?, *continued*

When I didn't have any food for four hours, I felt _____

because I needed _____.

When I already knew all the math problems in class, I felt _____

because I needed _____.

When I saw how messy the bathroom was, I felt _____

because I needed _____.

Requests vs. Demands

When we really want something and have a big feeling, it is easy to behave like a king or queen and start ordering people to do things. When we are really upset, we don't remember we actually can't *make* anyone do anything. They have to choose to do it. This is the difference between a demand ("you must do this!") and a request ("would you mind doing this?"). One is a demand and the other is a question.

People are usually more willing to help us when we ask instead of telling them what to do. This also means we are willing to hear no and compromise.

Let's take some demands and turn them into requests.

DEMANDING	ASKING
Stop bothering me!	Would you mind leaving me alone for five minutes?
Let me play more games!	
You have to buy that candy for me!	
Give me the ball!	

Requests vs. Demands, *continued*

DEMANDING	ASKING
I'm not going!	
Pick me up when I say so!	
Call them and tell them I'm not going!	
You can't play!	
You have to make me what I want to eat!	

OTHER PEOPLE FEEL ANGRY, TOO

Have you ever been told to imagine being in someone else's shoes? This is something we say to help us use empathy, which is our ability to imagine and understand how someone else feels.

Empathy is important, especially when anger is involved. Empathy lets us see the big picture, beyond the tunnel vision we get when we have a big emotion.

When we meet anger with more anger, everyone's anger level goes up and there is an eruption, like a volcano. We often meet anger with anger because we feel the urge to stand up for ourselves, protect our point of view, and let people know why our opinion is right. This makes the other person involved feel like doing the same thing.

When we meet anger with understanding, we are using empathy to pause and imagine how the other person may be feeling and what they may need. We can use this understanding to work together and help each other get what we both need or want.

When we feel angry, we can also feel stubborn. Anger can make us want to put our foot down and insist on doing things our way. Anger can also make us feel like we are in jail, stuck in a feeling we can't get free from. When we forgive ourselves and others, we set ourselves free from the anger jail. Most of the time, our friends and family are not trying to make us angry. They just have needs that are different from ours for the moment.

Inviting forgiveness in is like planting a seed of possibility. We are not forcing ourselves to forgive someone when we are not ready to forgive them yet. Instead, we imagine what forgiveness would look like and feel like, so we are readier to allow ourselves to feel it. Forgiveness allows us to see our truest wish for everyone (including ourselves): to be happy and peaceful.

When Anger Meets Anger

The following scenarios contain two people who are both angry or frustrated. The words in red are what they might say to each other when anger meets anger.

As you imagine yourself in these situations, circle an action you could take to calm yourself down. Then imagine a calm response directed toward the other person.

YOU NEVER LISTEN!   NEITHER DO YOU!

What could you do when you feel anger from what your sibling or friend said? (circle one)

- Stop and take a breath.
- Ask for a few minutes to calm down.

What would a *calm* response be? _____

_____

_____

STOP PLAYING VIDEO GAMES!   I DON'T WANT TO!
                                   YOU NEVER LET ME PLAY!

What could you do when you feel anger from what your parent said? (circle one)

- Pause the game and take two belly breaths.
- Pause the game and tell your mom or dad you need a minute or two before you can talk.
- Imagine how Mom or Dad feels and what they may need.

What would a *calm* response to their words be? _____

_____

_____

When Anger Meets Anger, *continued*

GIVE ME MY TOY BACK!   NO! I WANT TO PLAY WITH IT.

What could you do when you feel anger from what your sibling or friend said? (circle one)

- Walk away and return when you are calm.
- Tell a parent what's going on.
- Find something else fun to do and come back in five minutes to calmly ask for the toy again.

What would a *calm* response be when you return? _

_ _

_ _

When Anger Meets Understanding

We can use the new words we learned to describe our feelings and needs (see p. 110) and apply them to other people. Empathy is our ability to imagine how other people may be feeling and what they may need.

Use the feelings and needs lists for this activity.

FEELINGS LIST

- Bored
- Calm
- Confident
- Cranky
- Curious
- Disappointed
- Disconnected
- Embarrassed
- Excited
- Exhausted
- Fragile
- Frustrated
- Grateful
- Jealous
- Lonely
- Overwhelmed
- Panicked
- Quiet
- Refreshed
- Relaxed
- Relieved
- Restless
- Sad
- Surprised
- Worried

NEEDS LIST

- Air
- Appreciation
- Attention
- Celebration
- Choice
- Connection to friends and family
- Cooperation
- Ease
- Feeling able to do something well
- Food
- Hope
- Independence
- Joy
- Love
- Movement
- Organization
- Play
- Safety
- Shelter
- Sleep
- Stability
- To be challenged
- To be understood/to understand
- To express creativity
- To express yourself
- Trust
- Water

When Anger Meets Understanding, *continued*

Scenario 1: Mom comes into your room and sees a lot of clothes and toys on the floor. She says, "What a mess. You never clean your room."

What might Mom be feeling? _

What does Mom need or want? _

Scenario 2: Your classmates are talking while the teacher is trying to talk. Your teacher says, "Stop talking! You are all going to stay in for recess."

What might your teacher be feeling? _

What might your teacher need or want? _

Scenario 3: A friend gets out in a baseball game after you play a strong move. He says, "You hit the ball too hard. I should get another chance."

What might your friend be feeling? _

What might your friend need or want? _

When Anger Meets Forgiveness

Anger can be very stubborn. It may be hard to forgive someone for something they did, whether they meant to be hurtful or not.

In this activity, you will practice planting the seeds of forgiveness. They will slowly open your heart to truly forgiving yourself and the other people involved in a difficult situation.

Bring to mind a difficult situation you had with someone recently.

Think of something you did that may have caused anger, whether you meant it or not.

What might you have done to add to the other person's anger? _

_ _

_ _

When Anger Meets Forgiveness, *continued*

Now put a hand over your heart and think the words, *May I forgive myself and let it go.*

Now think of the other person involved and how they may be feeling guilty or being hard on themselves.

What might they be feeling bad about? _____

_____

Then say to yourself, *May he/she forgive him/herself. May he/she let it go.*

Now think of the anger you feel toward the other person.

What are you still angry at them about? _____

_____

With a hand on your heart, say to yourself, *May I forgive him/her. May I release him/her.*

Now think of the anger the other person may feel toward you.

What do you think they might still be angry at you about? _____

_____

With a hand on your heart, say to yourself, *May he/she forgive and release me.*

Lastly, with your eyes closed, imagine both of you forgiving each other and, with a hand on your heart, say to yourself, *May we forgive and release each other.*

What do you imagine doing as you see both of you forgiving and releasing each other? _ _ _ _ _ _ _ _

_ _

_ _

Who is someone you would like to forgive? _

After trying this activity, how did you feel? _

_ _

_ _

THE CHOICE IS MINE

You've made it to the final section of the workbook! I hope you feel like you now have lots of tools to help you manage your anger and choose new ways of responding when big feelings come up.

In this section, we'll focus on taking control of our attention and noticing our urges. We'll also continue to practice choosing new ways of thinking and new areas to focus on to help you feel happier and more appreciative of all you have.

In the first part of this section, you will get some practice directing your attention on purpose. Just as a director tells actors what to do in a play, you can direct your attention to different experiences, like breathing and listening. You will also get a chance to urge-surf. When you surf an urge, you watch an urge—to move or talk, for example—get really strong. Then you watch it pass by as you stay in your mindful body posture. With practice, urge surfing makes it easier to be in charge of your body and actions.

Practicing gratitude is like flexing a muscle. In order for gratitude to feel natural, you have to practice it as often as possible. When we are thankful, we remember all the people, opportunities, and things we have that make our lives great. When we remember the parts of ourselves that we are proud of or thankful for, we feel encouraged to keep acting in healthy ways.

When we are upset, it is easy to forget what brings us joy or takes us out of a cranky mood. If, when we are calm, we identify things that make us happy, we can create a list to look back on when we feel confused or grumpy. We will see that we can choose to do the things and be in the places that bring us calm and happiness.

In the last activity, you will imagine a day filled with *heartfulness*. Heartfulness is a feeling of friendliness that you send to yourself and others. You can send wishes to be happy, peaceful, and calm throughout the day. No one has to know you're doing it, as it is done silently.

Sending heartfulness helps you become more considerate and caring toward other people. It also helps you stay in a good mood. When you choose heartfulness, you help your mind stay open, friendly, and interested in how others feel.

Surf the Urge

Do you have urges? Of course you do! We all have urges, like the urge to eat when we are hungry or the urge to scratch an itch.

When we have an urge, we feel like we don't have a choice, but we do. If we act on all our urges, we can get distracted and feel unfocused. For example, you may feel restless in class and feel like you can't sit still. Or you may feel the urge to hit something when you are very angry.

For this activity, we are going to practice urge-surfing. We'll notice what it's like to sit very still and notice urges rise in us like an ocean wave. Then we'll watch them fall away as we choose to watch them instead of act on them.

MOUNTAIN POSTURE

1. Sit comfortably in a chair or on a couch.
2. Let your feet rest on the floor and your hands rest on your legs.
3. Feel your back straight and relaxed.
4. Set a timer for one minute to sit completely still in your pose.
5. You can think of your head like the peak of a mountain, your shoulders as the slopes, and your lower body as the base of the mountain.
6. Close your eyes and think of a beautiful mountain you've seen before or would like to see. Imagine you are just like that mountain now—still, sturdy, and strong.
7. As you watch urges to move, notice what the urge feels like. Is it a tingling, heat, or itchiness? Where do you feel the urge in your body? Continue to watch your urges for the full minute, then answer the questions below.

What urges did you notice? _

_ _

What did it feel like to urge-surf? _

_ _

Did you act on any urge? _____
_____

Where do you think you might practice urge-surfing in your daily life? _____
_____

How do you think urge-surfing might help you with anger? _____
_____
_____

Switching Attention on Purpose

Sometimes our attention can be like a puppy, running around in all directions and unable to focus on any one thing. With a little bit of practice, we can guide our puppy mind to focus on things we want to pay attention to, like playing an instrument or a sport, or listening to our teachers and friends. Being able to focus our attention helps us with learning, getting along with people, and calming ourselves when we are upset.

Look around the room slowly and notice something you have never noticed before. What is it?

Close your eyes and take three slow breaths, saying, "Breathing in, breathing out," silently to yourself.

Keeping your eyes closed, notice three sensations in your body (like heat or coolness, hunger or thirst, or something else).

What did you notice? _

_ _

_ _

Now close your eyes and listen for three different sounds.

What did you hear? _

_ _

_ _

What's the quietest sound you can hear? _

_ _

Lastly, think of someone you love or like a lot. Close your eyes and imagine them doing something that makes them feel happy, peaceful, and strong.

Who did you think about? _

_ _

Draw what you imagined them doing when they were happy, peaceful, and strong.

See how much control you have over what you think about and focus on? When you are at school or at home, notice when your mind is behaving like a puppy. Practice bringing it back to where you want it to be—with a lot of love, of course.

Gratitude for My Efforts

Taking time to be thankful is important. It is easy to think of things that are going wrong or that could be better, but it takes a little extra effort to think of things we are grateful for.

Practicing thankfulness takes time and commitment, just like learning an instrument or a sport. Being thankful helps us remember all the good things and people as well as our efforts to be kind, cooperative, and considerate. It also motivates us to keep doing our best because we realize how good it feels.

Let's take some time to think about all the people, things, and experiences we are grateful for.

Close your eyes and ask yourself:

What am I grateful to my family for? _____

_____

What am I grateful for having? _____

_____

What am I grateful for right now? _____

_____

Now, think about how your day has gone so far. Can you think of three things you are grateful to yourself for? For example, you may feel grateful to yourself for helping with chores or choosing a calm response to anger. No matter how small it is, write it down below.

Three of my actions I am grateful for today:

1. --

2. --

3. --

How does it feel to be thankful?

My Best Day Ever: Choosing Wisely

When we are grumpy, we may not feel like doing much at all. We may feel like staying inside by ourselves and staying mad for a while. However, it's important to choose to do things we enjoy and find relaxing. That way, we don't wallow in an unhappy state for too long. When we do things we enjoy, even if it's just for a short time, we keep ourselves happy and peaceful.

Whether it's listening to music or celebrating National Watermelon Day, let's discover some activities you enjoy and find relaxing. Read through the list of activities and circle the ones you like best. Then add three of your own.

RELAXING ACTIVITIES

Cooking with family

Taking my pet for a walk

Hanging out with a friend

Watching a movie

Listening to music

Playing board games

Reading a book

Taking a bath

What am I listening to?

FUN ACTIVITIES

There are many ways to have fun every day. Add three more fun activities to the list below.

I have fun . . .

Celebrating something

- -

Having a picnic

- -

Playing a sport

- -

Playing in the park

My Best Day Ever: Choosing Wisely, *continued*

What am I celebrating?

Close your eyes and imagine yourself doing something that makes you feel calm.

What did you imagine? _

_ _

_ _

Close your eyes and imagine yourself doing something fun.

What do you see? _

_ _

_ _

Heartfulness

Some days we wake up feeling groggy or cranky. Other days we wake up feeling excited and energized. With all our ups and downs, we can forget how much power we have to choose the way we respond to ourselves and others.

In this activity, we imagine sending friendliness and kindness to people throughout the day.

Draw a picture of someone you see when you wake up in the morning.

Now close your eyes and imagine sending them friendliness. You may imagine them having a healthy breakfast or a happy day.

Add a picture of you sending kindness and friendliness to this person.

Heartfulness, *continued*

Now think of someone you see at school. It could be a friend or a teacher. Close your eyes and imagine sending them friendliness or kindness. You could imagine them playing with their friends or doing something that makes them feel calm and relaxed.

Draw a picture of you sending them kindness.

Now imagine it is the end of a long, joyful day and you are snuggled in your bed. Close your eyes and send yourself friendliness and kindness. You may imagine yourself sleeping deeply or waking up feeling refreshed and happy.

Draw you sending yourself friendliness.

RESOURCES

Inward Bound Mindfulness Education (iBme)

www.ibme.info

Inward Bound is a nonprofit that offers mindfulness programming for youth and the parents and professionals in their lives. They also provide residential mindfulness retreats for adolescents.

Mindful Schools

www.mindfulschools.org

This organization offers virtual mindfulness training for educators and parents alike. They also offer a comprehensive mindfulness curriculum training to schools.

Peak Brain Institute

www.peakbraininstitute.com

This center for neurofeedback and mindfulness offers mindfulness courses for children in Culver City, California.

Stop, Breathe & Think

This is an app available for download on Android and Apple devices. It offers guided meditations and mindfulness practices tailored to children and adolescents. Its engaging audio and video content allows kids to provide feedback on how they feel in the moment. It offers a wide array of practice options based on how the child feels.

UCLA Mindful Awareness Research Center (MARC)

www.marc.ucla.edu

MARC offers six-week MAPs (Mindful Awareness Practices) classes that introduce adults to the foundations of mindfulness, including establishing a regular practice, regulation of difficult emotions, and cultivating positive emotional states.

BOOKS

Brainstorm by Daniel J. Siegel

This is a great book for adolescents and their parents. It provides information about the adolescent brain and ways of making the most of this developmental stage.

The Mindful Child by Susan Kaiser Greenland

This book provides activities parents can do with their children to foster mindfulness, self-awareness, emotional regulation, and present-moment awareness.

No-Drama Discipline by Daniel J. Siegel and Tina Payne Bryson

This book provides mindfulness-based discipline strategies that promote cooperation, learning from conflict, and compassion.

The Whole-Brain Child by Daniel J. Siegel and Tina Payne Bryson

This book describes best parenting practices based on current neuroscience research on the developing brain.

INDEX

ABOUT THE AUTHOR

For over 10 years, Samantha Snowden has worked with teens, families, and adults from all over the world. She started coaching teens with UCLA and worked in communities all over Los Angeles as a strengths-based coach and educator. Samantha has volunteered in Guatemala, Portugal, Spain, the UK, Sweden, and Peru providing community-based psychological services to youth and families.

Samantha has worked with some of the most prestigious and effective youth-empowerment programs, including the EduCare Foundation, Insight Seminars, the Canadian Alliance for Development Initiatives and Projects (CADIP), UCLA Mindful Awareness Research Center (MARC), UCLA Community Based Learning Program, and the UCLA Neuropsychiatric Institute, the Detox Center at Mount Sinai St. Luke's in New York City, as well as meditation centers both locally and abroad. She has designed and led school-based mindfulness programs for schools in Los Angeles as well as adult education programs abroad. She has also led online mindfulness courses for UnitedHealthcare's Moment Health Program.

She received her bachelor's degree in psychology from UCLA and her master's degree in clinical and educational psychology from Columbia University. She co-developed a mindfulness program at Columbia while being a researcher in the mindfulness lab. Additionally, Samantha has received training in behavioral neuroscience, guided imagery, yoga, and nutrition.

Samantha completed a certificate in mindfulness facilitation from the UCLA Mindful Awareness Research Center and trained with Mindful Schools and Inner Kids. She offers mindfulness coaching and facilitation for youth, adults, families, schools, and educators both in person and online. She is currently the international mindfulness coordinator for Peak Brain Institute.

NOTES